THIS BOOK BELONGS TO

START DATE

SHE READS TRUTH

CONTRIBUTORS

SPECIAL THANKS
Jessica Lamb
Rebecca Faires
Russ Ramsey
Kara Gause
Amanda Barnhart
Nate Shurden
Caleb Faires
Ellen Taylor

SUBSCRIPTION INQUIRIES
orders@shereadstruth.com

SHE READS TRUTH™

ISBN 978-1-952670-85-5

1 2 3 4 5 6 7 8 9 10

Though the dates and locations in this book have been carefully researched, scholars disagree on many of these topics.

Research support provided by Logos Bible Software™. Learn more at logos.com.

THE PSALMS OF ASCENT

SONGS FOR THE JOURNEY

SHE READS TRUTH

These songs for the journey are words to set our hearts on as we go.

Raechel Myers
FOUNDER

Our family has lived in Tennessee now for almost two decades. Our babies were born here, our work is here, and yes, my vegetable garden is here. Yet there is something about "going home" to the place that raised us. My husband and I grew up together in Michigan, and his parents still live there. When we say "we're going home," it means we're headed to Michigan. Every January and July our family packs our bags and our traditional airplane snacks (Chex Mix for me, Nerd Clusters and other nonsense for everyone else) and begin our journey to our hometown. It's part of the rhythm of our lives. We look forward to it, count on it, and arrange our calendars around it.

The Old Testament people of God had their annual trips too. Wherever they lived the rest of the year, no matter how far, many traveled to the capital city of Jerusalem—a high point in the land—every spring to celebrate Passover. Likewise, each summer they would make the journey for the Festival of Weeks and again in autumn for the Festival of Shelters.

These weren't just family reunions. These feasts, these rhythms, were a way of walking through the calendar of redemption every year, emblazoning the history of their faith on their memory and their feet. Simultaneously leaving their homes and going to the home of their faith, the Jewish people were regularly reminded that God was their dwelling place, no matter where they rested their heads.

Psalms 120–134 are known as the Psalms of Ascent (or Songs of Ascent, or some combination thereof, depending on which Bible translation you use). They are a series of short songs used to divide the journey, each focusing on essential aspects of the life of a child of God, and sung by worshipers as they made this climb to Jerusalem.

These songs for the journey are words to set our hearts on as we go. They are written to help us feel what we are meant to feel—the blunt force of tragedy, the wonder of beauty, the longing for rescue, the indignation that opposes injustice and evil. They are a way for us to inscribe the history of our faith on our own memory and feet.

Our team is so glad to share the scriptures in this Reading Guide with you. We love how communal the Psalms of Ascent are—they are meant to be read and studied and recited together as a community of men and women drawing nearer to their God. We hope you'll do just that. Invite someone to study these fifteen psalms with you (bring some Chex Mix along if you like), and engage with the questions we've presented. Most of all, be reminded that, as believers, God is our dwelling place—both now and forever.

DESIGN *on* PURPOSE

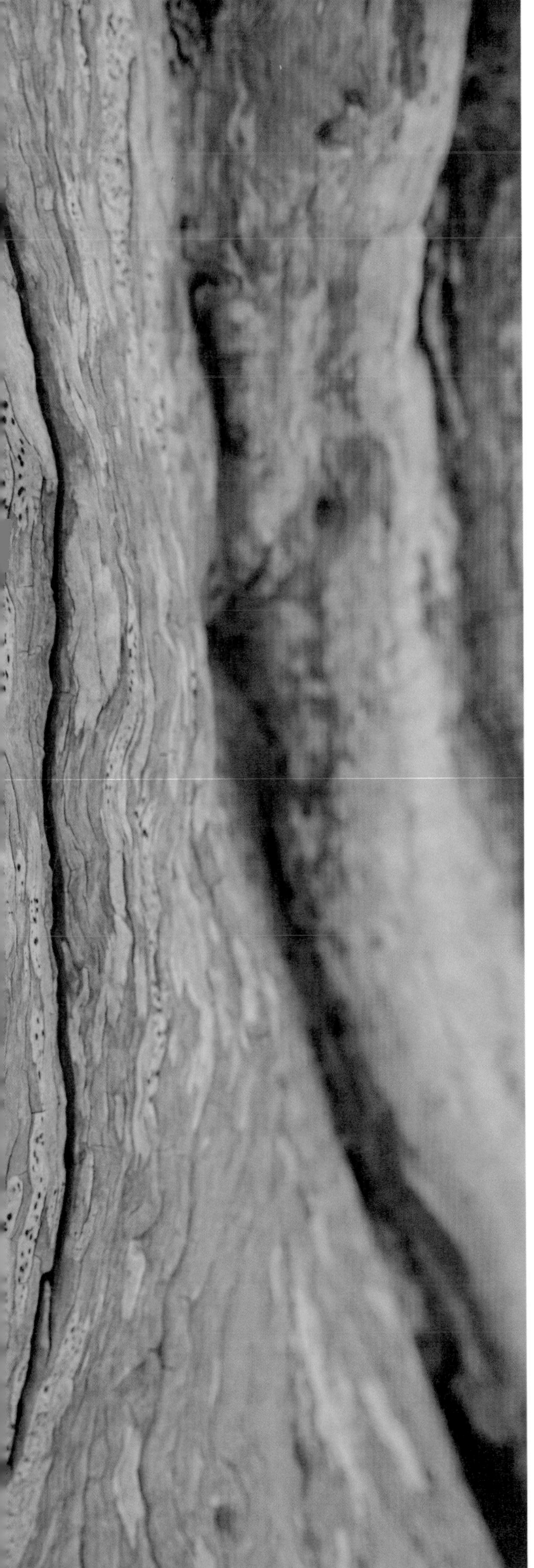

At She Reads Truth, we believe in pairing the inherently beautiful Word of God with the aesthetic beauty it deserves. Each of our resources is thoughtfully and artfully designed to highlight the beauty, goodness, and truth of Scripture in a way that reflects the themes of each curated reading plan.

Whenever we read the Psalms of Ascent, they can encourage us no matter where we are in our spiritual journey. We emphasized this idea in the design of this Daily Reading Guide by showcasing an earthy color palette and images of repeating patterns found in natural landscapes. The photography highlights these organic patterns to call out the highs and lows of life—and the God who is constant through them all.

HOW TO USE THIS BOOK

She Reads Truth is a community of women dedicated to reading the Word of God every day. In **The Psalms of Ascent** reading plan, we will receive instruction and encouragement for the difficult and hopeful parts of our experience as Christians.

READ & REFLECT

The Psalms of Ascent book focuses primarily on Scripture, with added features to come alongside your time with God's Word.

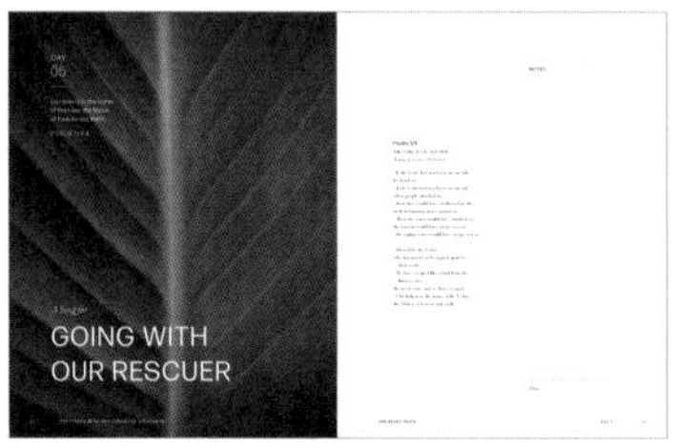

SCRIPTURE READING

Designed for a Monday start, this book presents daily readings from the book of Psalms, specifically the Psalms of Ascent.

REFLECTION QUESTIONS

Each weekday features questions and space for personal reflection.

COMMUNITY & CONVERSATION

You can start reading this book at any time! If you want to join women from Nashville to Norway as they read along with you, the She Reads Truth community will start Day 1 of **The Psalms of Ascent** on Monday, June 3, 2024.

SHE READS TRUTH APP

For added community and conversation, join us in **The Psalms of Ascent** reading plan on the She Reads Truth app. You can use the app to participate in community discussion and more.

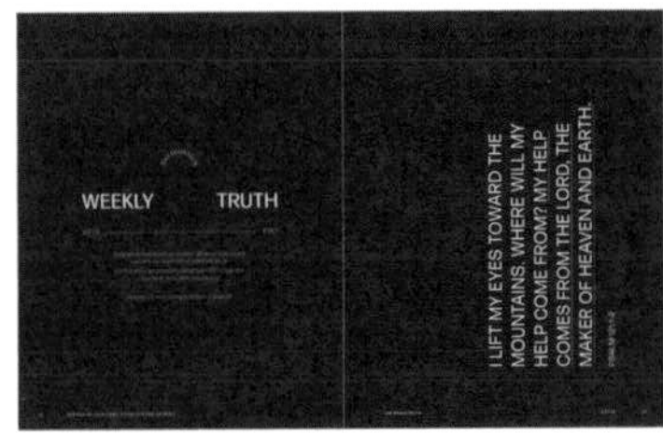

GRACE DAY

Use Saturdays to catch up on your reading, pray, and rest in the presence of the Lord.

WEEKLY TRUTH

Sundays are set aside for Scripture memorization.

See tips for memorizing Scripture on page 96.

EXTRAS

This book features additional tools to help you gain a deeper understanding of the text.

Find a complete list of extras on page 11.

SHEREADSTRUTH.COM

The Psalms of Ascent reading plan and community discussion will also be available at SheReadsTruth.com as the community reads each day. Invite your family, friends, and neighbors to read along with you!

SHE READS TRUTH PODCAST

Subscribe to the She Reads Truth Podcast, and join our founders and their guests each week as they talk about what you'll read in the week ahead.

Podcast episodes 228–230 for ***The Psalms of Ascent*** *series release on Mondays beginning June 3, 2024.*

TABLE

of

CONTENTS

KEY —— VERSE

MY HELP COMES FROM THE LORD, THE MAKER OF HEAVEN AND EARTH.

PSALM 121:2

She Reads

THE PSALMS OF ASCENT

THE PSALMS OF ASCENT

In the Old Testament, God commanded the Israelite people to uphold specific practices as regular reminders of their identity as the people of God. This included instructions to gather together three specific times each year for different festivals. The nation first held these gatherings at the site of the tabernacle, the movable tent that served as a temporary dwelling place for the presence of God. After the completion of the first temple in 960 BC, Jerusalem became the center of worship and gathering for the nation. Three times each year, Israelites from around the region made the journey to Jerusalem to celebrate God's appointed festivals (see "The Three Pilgrimage Festivals" on page 30).

Jerusalem sits at a high elevation point in the region, so to go to Jerusalem was to go up to Jerusalem. Psalms 120-134 were likely sung by the people as they climbed, moving the travelers toward their destination with intention, beauty, and instruction. These psalms became known as the Psalms of Ascent, a way to actively remember who God is and His promises while making the journey.

THE ACT OF REMEMBERING

Zakar is the main Hebrew root used in the Old Testament for concepts related to remembrance and memory. While the word can mean recalling the past, it also carries a greater weight. Zakar asks us to do something with our memories, using the past to inform our present thoughts, feelings, and actions.

God knows how quickly our actions follow our forgetting. When we don't remember what is true, we can't walk in accordance with what God has instructed.

While followers of Jesus are no longer instructed to physically pilgrimage to Jerusalem, the Christian life has its own spiritual ascents—times of growth, recovering from loss, or deepening of faith. We make these climbs with our sight set on the home we have in God's presence. The Psalms of Ascent give us clear depictions and words to sing, pray, or speak over our journey to remember what is true when the road looks steep. They help us embrace life's difficulties as a part of the journey, singing from one bend in the trail to another—because even when the road is hard, we are bound for glory. The act of remembering is a part of discipleship, of pairing our steps with truth in our minds and hearts to continually trust God's faithfulness along the way.

IN THIS READING PLAN

Over three weeks, we will read through Psalms 120-134, looking at the example of singing in ascent as a model of encouragement for our own formation in the Christian life. Each day, we'll read one psalm. Following the reading, a daily blurb will summarize the song and the posture it is meant to provide for the singer along with reflection questions, inviting you to consider how the psalm might shape your own life with Christ.

PSALM 120:1

IN MY DISTRESS I CALLED TO THE LORD, AND HE ANSWERED ME.

A SONG FOR GOING IN PEACE

Day 01 — *Week 01*

NOTES

Psalm 120

A CRY FOR TRUTH AND PEACE

A song of ascents.

1 In my distress I called to the LORD,
and he answered me.
2 "LORD, rescue me from lying lips
and a deceitful tongue."

3 What will he give you,
and what will he do to you,
you deceitful tongue?
4 A warrior's sharp arrows
with burning charcoal!

5 What misery that I have stayed in Meshech,
that I have lived among the tents of Kedar!
6 I have dwelt too long
with those who hate peace.
7 I am for peace; but when I speak,
they are for war.

____ / ____ / ____

Date

DAY

01

PSALM 120

This is a song for a person who is stirred to leave a broken world in search of a place where peace reigns. Dissatisfaction with present circumstances causes us to yearn for something more, and it is that desire that motivates us to get up from where we are and seek a better way.

01

In what areas of your life are you searching for peace?

02

How can you move toward God as a source of peace in those places?

DAY 02

A SONG FOR

GOING WHILE PROTECTED

THE LORD PROTECTS YOU; THE LORD IS A SHELTER RIGHT BY YOUR SIDE.

Psalm 121:5

WEEK 01

NOTES

Psalm 121

THE LORD OUR PROTECTOR

A song of ascents.

1 I lift my eyes toward the mountains.
Where will my help come from?
2 My help comes from the LORD,
the Maker of heaven and earth.

3 He will not allow your foot to slip;
your Protector will not slumber.
4 Indeed, the Protector of Israel
does not slumber or sleep.

5 The LORD protects you;
the LORD is a shelter right by your side.
6 The sun will not strike you by day
or the moon by night.

7 The LORD will protect you from all harm;
he will protect your life.
8 The LORD will protect your coming and going
both now and forever.

_____ / _____ / _____

Date

DAY

02

PSALM 121

This song is sung by someone confident in the Lord's protection in multiple ways, certain that God protects their whole life from danger and guards their individual steps. The journey described begins with eyes fixed on the One who will protect the traveler along the way, speaking what is true of God both now and forever.

01

What statements in this psalm about God's protection have you experienced?

02

Where do you feel you need God's protection most right now? How does this psalm help you see His protection in your present circumstances?

WEEK 01 — DAY 03

A Song for GOING HOME

I rejoiced with those who said to me, "Let's go to the house of the LORD."

PSALM 122:1

NOTES

Psalm 122

A PRAYER FOR JERUSALEM

A song of ascents. Of David.

1 I rejoiced with those who said to me,
"Let's go to the house of the LORD."
2 Our feet were standing
within your gates, Jerusalem—

3 Jerusalem, built as a city should be,
solidly united,
4 where the tribes, the LORD's tribes, go up
to give thanks to the name of the LORD.
(This is an ordinance for Israel.)
5 There, thrones for judgment are placed,
thrones of the house of David.

6 Pray for the well-being of Jerusalem:
"May those who love you be secure;
7 may there be peace within your walls,
security within your fortresses."
8 Because of my brothers and friends,
I will say, "May peace be in you."
9 Because of the house of the LORD our God,
I will pursue your prosperity.

____ / ____ / ____

Date

DAY

03

PSALM 122

In this song, the singer experiences a sense of homecoming when they enter Jerusalem. It describes the joy of feeling like we have arrived in a safe place of God's peace and protection, a homecoming to where we belong. Now, we do not need to take a trip to arrive at God's dwelling place; we need only to remember the living and active Spirit of God to be reminded that we are home in Him.

01

What other scriptures, songs, or memories remind you that God is your comfort and home?

02

Write a prayer over your home, hometown, or the city you currently live in. Pray for its well-being, asking God to be the true comfort and peace in that place.

DAY 04

GOING IN GOD'S FAVOR

I LIFT MY EYES TO YOU,
THE ONE ENTHRONED IN HEAVEN.

Psalm 123:1

WEEK 01

NOTES

Psalm 123

LOOKING FOR GOD'S FAVOR

A song of ascents.

1 I lift my eyes to you,
the one enthroned in heaven.
2 Like a servant's eyes on his master's hand,
like a servant girl's eyes on her mistress's hand,
so our eyes are on the LORD our God
until he shows us favor.

3 Show us favor, LORD, show us favor,
for we've had more than enough contempt.
4 We've had more than enough
scorn from the arrogant
and contempt from the proud.

___ / ___ / ___

Date

DAY

04

PSALM 123

This song is a reminder of where our help comes from, not only in protection from physical harm, but in the face of scorn, contempt, and pride. The song prompts the singer to hope in God's favor no matter what the journey brings.

01

What voices of scorn and contempt exist in your life? How do they distract you from following God?

02

How could you look to God in those areas?

EXTRA

THE THREE PILGRIMAGE FESTIVALS

In the Old Testament, God commands that His people gather together three specific times each year for different festivals. Here are the three festivals God's people celebrated in Jerusalem and how they honored God in the gathering.

PASSOVER AND THE FESTIVAL OF UNLEAVENED BREAD

Hebrew Word: Pesach

SEASON
Spring

COMMEMORATES
God sparing the firstborn sons of Israel and the nation's deliverance from Egypt

TRADITIONS
Present food offerings to God and eat unleavened bread for seven days.
Lv 23:5-8; Nm 28:16-25

FESTIVAL OF WEEKS (PENTECOST)

Hebrew Word: Shavuot

SEASON
Summer

COMMEMORATES
The harvest and, later in history, God's giving of the law at Mount Sinai

TRADITIONS
Give the firstfruits of the wheat harvest in proportion to what the Lord gave in the harvest.
Dt 16:9-12

FESTIVAL OF SHELTERS (FEAST OF TABERNACLES)

Hebrew Word: Sukkot

SEASON
Fall

COMMEMORATES
Israel dwelling in tents in the wilderness after God brought them out of Egypt

TRADITIONS
Present daily food offerings for eight days, rest on the first and eighth days of the feast, and live in makeshift dwellings.
Lv 23:33-44; Nm 29:12-40

DAY

05

Our help is in the name
of the LORD, the Maker
of heaven and earth.

PSALM 124:8

A Song for

GOING WITH OUR RESCUER

NOTES

Psalm 124

THE LORD IS ON OUR SIDE

A song of ascents. Of David.

1 If the LORD had not been on our side—
let Israel say—
2 if the LORD had not been on our side
when people attacked us,
3 then they would have swallowed us alive
in their burning anger against us.
4 Then the water would have engulfed us;
the torrent would have swept over us;
5 the raging water would have swept over us.

6 Blessed be the LORD,
who has not let us be ripped apart by
their teeth.
7 We have escaped like a bird from the
hunter's net;
the net is torn, and we have escaped.
8 Our help is in the name of the LORD,
the Maker of heaven and earth.

/ /

Date

DAY

05

PSALM 124

This song praises God as the true rescuer who saves His people, the One who has protected Israel from being overcome. This singer reflects and credits deliverance to the Lord in the face of each and every disaster that could have taken place.

01

Where are some places in your life that you currently feel fear or danger?

02

How does this song model how we can respond to danger?

GRACE DAY

Take this day to catch up on your reading, pray, and rest in the presence of the Lord.

Day Six

He will not allow your foot to slip; your Protector will not slumber.

PSALM 121:3

Week One

DAY SEVEN

WEEKLY TRUTH

WEEK ONE

Scripture is God-breathed and true. When we memorize it, we carry His Word with us wherever we go.

For this study, we will memorize Psalm 121:1-2 together. This week, we'll memorize verse 1.

See tips for memorizing Scripture on page 96.

I LIFT MY EYES TOWARD THE MOUNTAINS. WHERE WILL MY HELP COME FROM? MY HELP COMES FROM THE LORD, THE MAKER OF HEAVEN AND EARTH.

PSALM 121:1–2

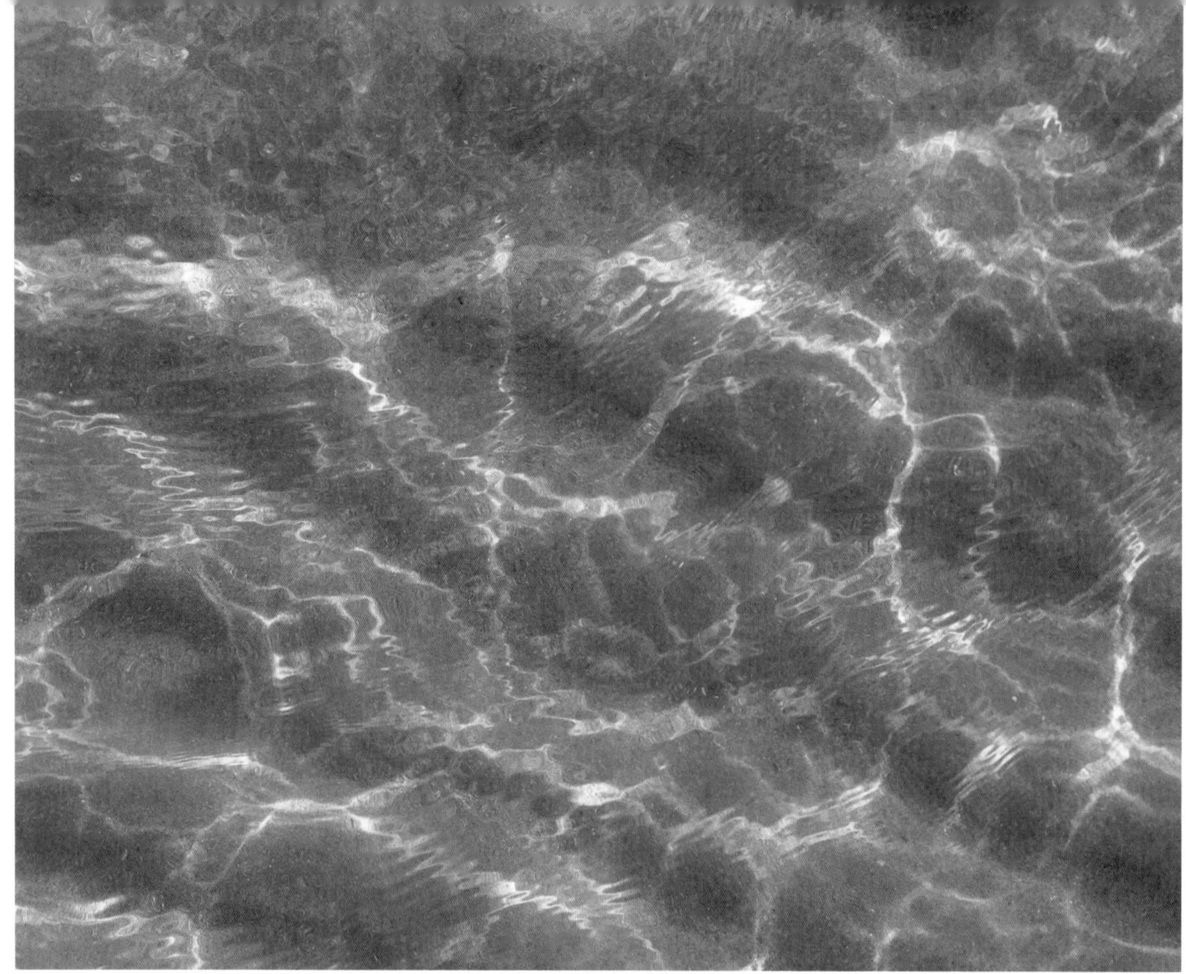

Day 08 *Week 02*

A Song for

GOING WITH TRUST IN THE LORD

Those who trust in the LORD are like Mount Zion.
It cannot be shaken; it remains forever.

PSALM 125:1

NOTES

Psalm 125

ISRAEL'S STABILITY

A song of ascents.

1 Those who trust in the LORD are like
Mount Zion.
It cannot be shaken; it remains forever.
2 The mountains surround Jerusalem
and the LORD surrounds his people,
both now and forever.

3 The scepter of the wicked will not remain
over the land allotted to the righteous,
so that the righteous will not apply their
hands to injustice.
4 Do what is good, LORD, to the good,
to those whose hearts are upright.
5 But as for those who turn aside to
crooked ways,
the LORD will banish them with
the evildoers.
Peace be with Israel.

/ /

Date

DAY

08

PSALM 125

This is a humble song acknowledging that the righteousness of God is the only path out of the company of evil and toward the goodness of His presence. The song encourages the singer to remember God's goodness by asking Him to act according to His character throughout the journey.

01

What is the outcome of those who trust in the Lord?

02

What scriptures, songs, or stories in your life remind you to trust in the Lord?

DAY 09

A SONG FOR

GOING WITH JOY

THOSE WHO SOW IN TEARS WILL
REAP WITH SHOUTS OF JOY.

Psalm 126:5

WEEK 02

NOTES

Psalm 126

ZION'S RESTORATION

A song of ascents.

1 When the LORD restored the fortunes
of Zion,
we were like those who dream.
2 Our mouths were filled with laughter then,
and our tongues with shouts of joy.
Then they said among the nations,
"The LORD has done great things for them."
3 The LORD had done great things for us;
we were joyful.

4 Restore our fortunes, LORD,
like watercourses in the Negev.
5 Those who sow in tears
will reap with shouts of joy.
6 Though one goes along weeping,
carrying the bag of seed,
he will surely come back with shouts of joy,
carrying his sheaves.

___ / ___ / ___

Date

DAY

09

PSALM 126

The ascent holds both sorrow and joy. This song uses the memory of hardships as encouragement to remember that joy is worth the journey. And with that hope, this song calls the singer to be confident God will continue to use sadness to bring a better joy as they press forward.

01

What makes it hard for you to remember or experience joy when you feel sorrowful?

02

In what area of your life do you most need to be reminded of joy?

DAY

10

In vain you get up early and stay up late, working hard to have enough food—yes, he gives sleep to the one he loves.

PSALM 127:2

A Song for

GOING WITH GOD'S PROVISION

NOTES

Psalm 127

THE BLESSING OF THE LORD

A song of ascents. Of Solomon.

1 Unless the LORD builds a house,
its builders labor over it in vain;
unless the LORD watches over a city,
the watchman stays alert in vain.
2 In vain you get up early and stay up late,
working hard to have enough food—
yes, he gives sleep to the one he loves.

3 Sons are indeed a heritage from the LORD,
offspring, a reward.
4 Like arrows in the hand of a warrior
are the sons born in one's youth.
5 Happy is the man who has filled his quiver
with them.
They will never be put to shame
when they speak with their enemies at the
city gate.

___/___/___

Date

DAY

10

PSALM 127

The ascent provides time to reflect on God's provision. In counting up the things the psalmist holds dear, the song tells of God's care for His people with praise and gratitude.

01

In what areas of your life are you the builder or protector?

02

How can you remember God's provision in those places?

MAP

THE JOURNEY HOME

Three times a year, God's people traveled from the surrounding regions and gathered in Jerusalem to celebrate feasts commemorating God's faithfulness. This map illustrates the general routes those living throughout the region may have taken on their ascent to the city.

Some scholars have concluded that ancient pilgrims may not have used the established roadways on their entire journey and instead chose to travel more difficult routes for some of the trip as a part of their spiritual experience.

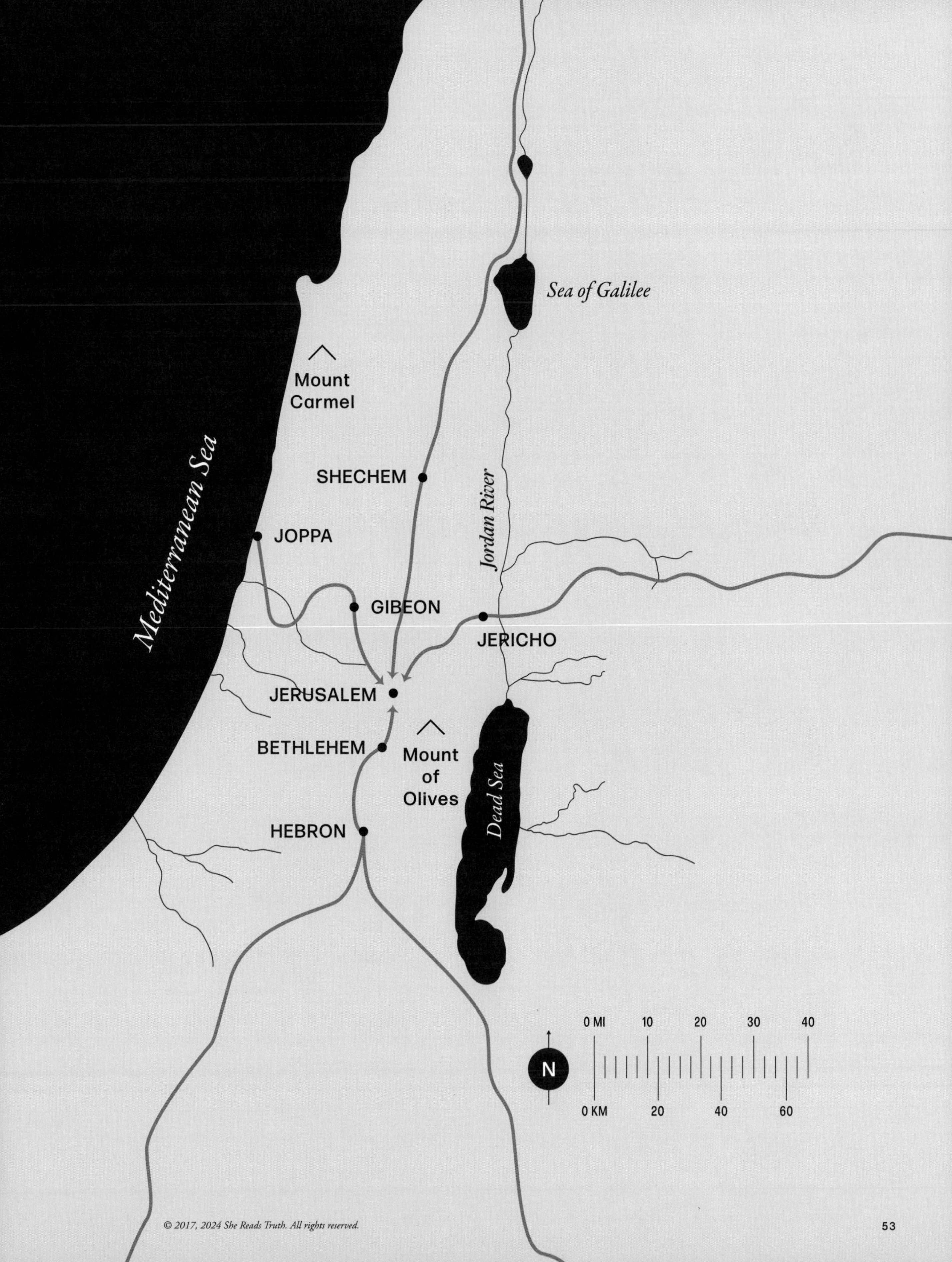
Sea of Galilee
Mount Carmel
Mediterranean Sea
SHECHEM
Jordan River
JOPPA
GIBEON
JERICHO
JERUSALEM
BETHLEHEM
Mount of Olives
Dead Sea
HEBRON
N
0 MI
10
20
30
40
0 KM
20
40
60

DAY 11

A SONG FOR

GOING IN OBEDIENCE

HOW HAPPY IS EVERYONE WHO FEARS THE LORD, WHO WALKS IN HIS WAYS!

Psalm 128:1

WEEK 02

NOTES

Psalm 128

BLESSINGS FOR THOSE WHO FEAR GOD

A song of ascents.

1 How happy is everyone who fears the LORD,
who walks in his ways!
2 You will surely eat
what your hands have worked for.
You will be happy,
and it will go well for you.
3 Your wife will be like a fruitful vine
within your house,
your children, like young olive trees
around your table.
4 In this very way
the man who fears the LORD
will be blessed.

5 May the LORD bless you from Zion,
so that you will see the prosperity of Jerusalem
all the days of your life
6 and will see your children's children!
Peace be with Israel.

/ /

Date

DAY

11

PSALM 128

The song focuses on how living according to God's wisdom brings joy, peace, and prosperity. Like a traveler walks along the right path in order to reach their destination, our walking in obedience leads to His goodness.

01

What questions come to mind when you read about fearing the Lord?

02

Where in your life do you need to be reminded of the goodness of obeying God?

PSALM 129:4

THE LORD IS RIGHTEOUS; HE HAS CUT THE ROPES OF THE WICKED.

A SONG FOR GOING WITH CONFIDENCE IN THE LORD

Day 12 — *Week 02*

NOTES

Psalm 129

PROTECTION OF THE OPPRESSED

A song of ascents.

1 Since my youth they have often attacked me—
let Israel say—
2 since my youth they have often attacked me,
but they have not prevailed against me.
3 Plowmen plowed over my back;
they made their furrows long.
4 The LORD is righteous;
he has cut the ropes of the wicked.

5 Let all who hate Zion
be driven back in disgrace.
6 Let them be like grass on the rooftops,
which withers before it grows up
7 and can't even fill the hands of the reaper
or the arms of the one who binds sheaves.
8 Then none who pass by will say,
"May the LORD's blessing be on you.
We bless you in the name of the LORD."

_____ / _____ / _____

Date

DAY

12

PSALM 129

This psalm addresses Israel's long history of wars with neighboring armies and the oppression of foreign invaders. In reflecting on these injustices, the song recalls a confidence in the Lord as the One who conquers all evil.

01

How does this psalm describe how God deals with evil in the world?

02

How does going in confidence in the Lord change how you live?

EXTRA

A SONG FOR THE JOURNEY

Though we may not be physically journeying to Jerusalem, we all have our own journeys in life with unique ups and downs. We all need encouraging reminders that God is with us along the way. Use this template based on Psalm 123 to write your own song for the journey.

PSALM 123	PROMPT	*Fill in your song for the journey below.*
1 I lift my eyes to you, the one enthroned in heaven.	*Where are you inclined to look for help?*	
2 Like a servant's eyes on his master's hand, like a servant girl's eyes on her mistress's hand,	*How do you stay connected and dependent on God?*	
so our eyes are on the LORD our God until he shows us favor.	*Where do you direct your eyes as you walk through life?*	
3 Show us favor, LORD, show us favor,	*What is your request?*	
for we've had more than enough contempt.	*What have you had enough of?*	
4 We've had more than enough scorn from the arrogant and contempt from the proud.	*What else do you need freedom from?*	

GRACE DAY

Take this day to catch up on your reading, pray, and rest in the presence of the Lord.

Day Thirteen

The LORD had done great things for us; we were joyful.

PSALM 126:3

Week Two

DAY FOURTEEN

WEEKLY TRUTH

WEEK — TWO

Scripture is God-breathed and true. When we memorize it, we carry His Word with us wherever we go.

For this study, we are memorizing Psalm 121:1-2 together. This week, we'll memorize verse 2.

See tips for memorizing Scripture on page 96.

I LIFT MY EYES TOWARD THE MOUNTAINS. WHERE WILL MY HELP COME FROM? MY HELP COMES FROM THE LORD, THE MAKER OF HEAVEN AND EARTH.

PSALM 121:1–2

DAY

15

I wait for the LORD; I wait
and put my hope in his word.

PSALM 130:5

A Song for

GOING WITH HOPE

NOTES

Psalm 130

AWAITING REDEMPTION

A song of ascents.

1 Out of the depths I call to you, LORD!
2 Lord, listen to my voice;
let your ears be attentive
to my cry for help.

3 LORD, if you kept an account of iniquities,
Lord, who could stand?
4 But with you there is forgiveness,
so that you may be revered.

5 I wait for the LORD; I wait
and put my hope in his word.
6 I wait for the Lord
more than watchmen for the morning—
more than watchmen for the morning.

7 Israel, put your hope in the LORD.
For there is faithful love with the LORD,
and with him is redemption in abundance.
8 And he will redeem Israel
from all its iniquities.

___ / ___ / ___

Date

DAY

15

PSALM 130

In order to ascend to Jerusalem, the traveler had to come up from a lower place. As the psalmist imagines being pulled back down by the weight of sin, they call on the hope that God's faithful love will redeem their iniquities. This song is rooted in abundance, knowing that God will receive reverence and glory for the redemption to come.

01

What does the singer do when faced with their iniquity? How does the song describe how God handles iniquity?

02

How can you use the words and truth in this song when dealing with your own sin?

DAY 16

A SONG FOR

GOING IN HUMILITY

ISRAEL, PUT YOUR HOPE IN THE LORD,

BOTH NOW AND FOREVER.

Psalm 131:3

WEEK 03

NOTES

Psalm 131

A CHILDLIKE SPIRIT

A song of ascents. Of David.

1 Lord, my heart is not proud;
my eyes are not haughty.
I do not get involved with things
too great or too wondrous for me.
2 Instead, I have calmed and quieted my soul
like a weaned child with its mother;
my soul is like a weaned child.

3 Israel, put your hope in the Lord,
both now and forever.

/ /

Date

DAY

16

PSALM 131

This song singularly focuses on a humble heart as the best posture for ascending. Not arrogantly striving to know the way better than God, the song reminds the singer to rest in their trust in Him. Instead of pride, God gives the quiet peace of a connected soul.

01

How does this psalm describe a humble heart?

02

Where do you feel pride pulling you away from God's presence?

WEEK 03 — DAY 17

A Song for GOING TO HIS PRESENCE

Let's go to his dwelling place;
let's worship at his footstool.

PSALM 132:7

Psalm 132

DAVID AND ZION CHOSEN

A song of ascents.

1 LORD, remember David
and all the hardships he endured,
2 and how he swore an oath to the LORD,
making a vow to the Mighty One of Jacob:
3 "I will not enter my house
or get into my bed,
4 I will not allow my eyes to sleep
or my eyelids to slumber
5 until I find a place for the LORD,
a dwelling for the Mighty One of Jacob."

6 We heard of the ark in Ephrathah;
we found it in the fields of Jaar.
7 Let's go to his dwelling place;
let's worship at his footstool.
8 Rise up, LORD, come to your resting place,
you and your powerful ark.
9 May your priests be clothed with righteousness,
and may your faithful people shout for joy.
10 For the sake of your servant David,
do not reject your anointed one.

11 The LORD swore an oath to David,
a promise he will not abandon:
"I will set one of your offspring
on your throne.
12 If your sons keep my covenant
and my decrees that I will teach them,
their sons will also sit on your throne forever."

13 For the LORD has chosen Zion;
he has desired it for his home:
14 "This is my resting place forever;
I will make my home here
because I have desired it.
15 I will abundantly bless its food;
I will satisfy its needy with bread.
16 I will clothe its priests with salvation,
and its faithful people will shout for joy.
17 There I will make a horn grow for David;
I have prepared a lamp for my anointed one.
18 I will clothe his enemies with shame,
but the crown he wears will be glorious."

DAY

17

PSALM 132

This song both remembers God's purpose in making His dwelling place in Jerusalem and looks to a promised future of God's presence in abundance. In praising God for bringing Israel through hardship, the song reveals that to truly be home is to be with God.

01

When you look back on seasons of hardship or struggle, what do you remember longing for in those circumstances?

02

How can you invite God's presence into current areas of hardship?

For those who trust God's changeless love build on the rock that will not move.

IF YOU BUT TRUST IN GOD TO GUIDE YOU

1 If you but trust in God to guide you and place your
2 On - ly be still and wait His plea - sure in cheer - ful
3 Sing, pray, and keep His ways un - swerv- ing, of - fer your
con - fi - dence in Him, you'll find Him al - ways there be - side you
hope with heart con - tent. He fills your needs to ful - lest mea - sure
ser - vice faith - ful - ly, and trust His Word; though un - de - serv - ing,
to give you hope and strength with - in; for those who trust God's
with what dis - cern - ing love has sent; doubt not our in - most
you'll find His prom - ise true to be. God nev - er will for -
change - less love build on the rock that will not move.
wants are known to Him who chose us for His own.
sake in need the soul that trusts in Him in - deed.

TEXT AND TUNE —— GEORG NEUMARK, 1641 AND 1657

DAY 18

GOING WITH COMMUNITY

FOR THERE THE LORD HAS APPOINTED
THE BLESSING—LIFE FOREVERMORE.

Psalm 133:3

WEEK 03

NOTES

Psalm 133

LIVING IN HARMONY

A song of ascents. Of David.

1 How delightfully good
when brothers live together in harmony!
2 It is like fine oil on the head,
running down on the beard,
running down Aaron's beard
onto his robes.
3 It is like the dew of Hermon
falling on the mountains of Zion.
For there the LORD has appointed
the blessing—
life forevermore.

____ / ____ / ____

Date

DAY

18

PSALM 133

This song celebrates how good it is when God's people live in unity, comparing this harmony to the holiness of Aaron's anointing as a priest. God's blessing rests over this kind of living, giving encouragement to those on their journey longing for unity in their own lives.

01

What are some examples in your life and relationships of living in harmony?

02

How can you celebrate those people in your life today?

Day 19 *Week 03*

A Song for

GOING WITH PRAISE

May the LORD, Maker of heaven and earth, bless you from Zion.

PSALM 134:3

NOTES

Psalm 134

CALL TO EVENING WORSHIP

A song of ascents.

1 Now bless the LORD,
all you servants of the LORD
who stand in the LORD's house at night!
2 Lift up your hands in the holy place
and bless the LORD!

3 May the LORD,
Maker of heaven and earth,
bless you from Zion.

___ / ___ / ___

Date

DAY

19

PSALM 134

The song moves the traveler to join in communal worship as they arrive with other travelers in the house of the Lord. They lift holy hands together, praising God with one voice. Though the journey may have been long and night has fallen, there is an atmosphere of arrival. Hear their invitation: worship the Lord!

01

How do you practice worship in your own life?

02

Use this space to write your own prayer of worship, praising God for wherever you are in your own journey.

GRACE DAY

Take this day to catch up on your reading, pray, and rest in the presence of the Lord.

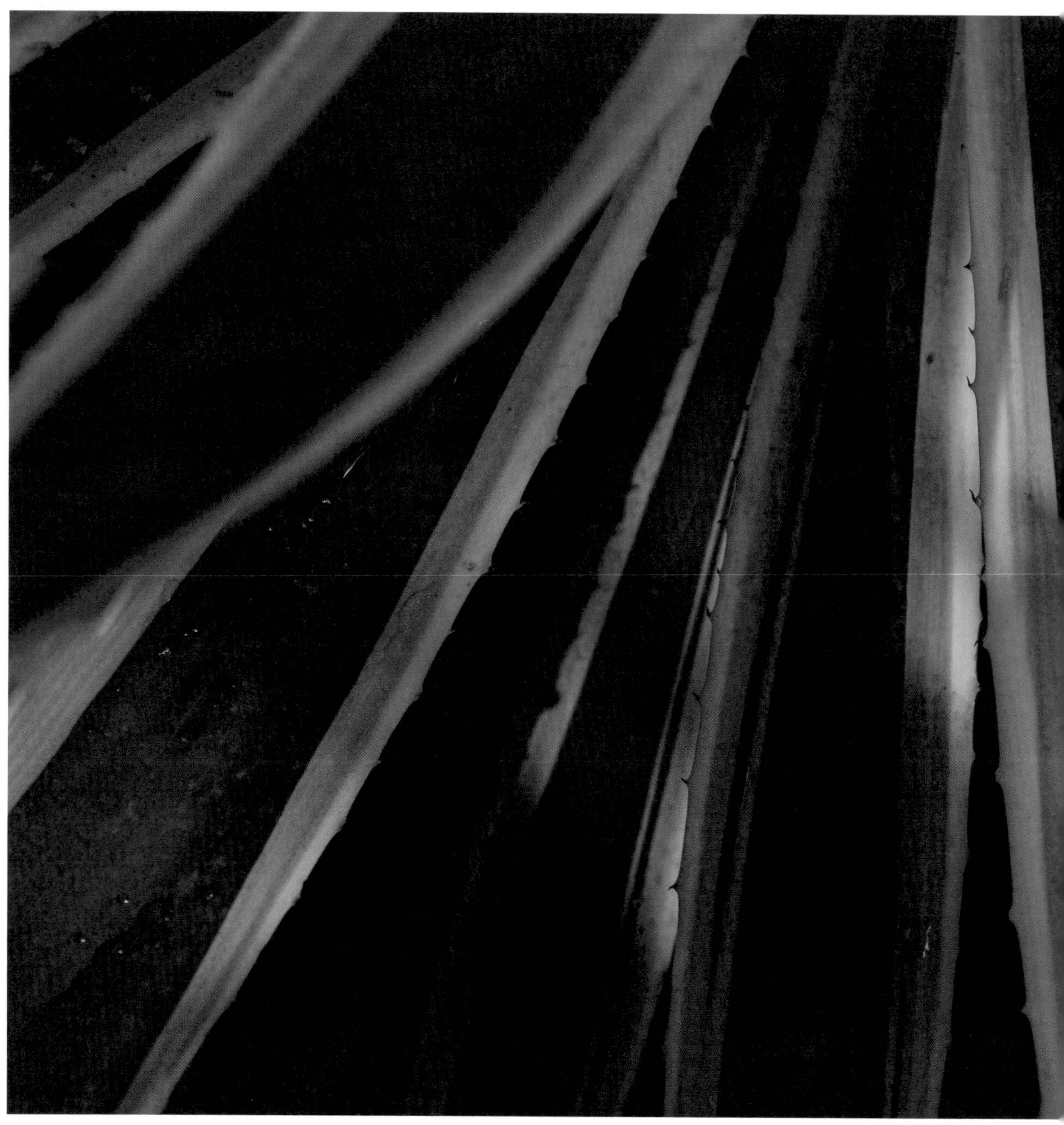

Day Twenty

Israel, put your hope in the LORD. For there is faithful love with the LORD, and with him is redemption in abundance.

PSALM 130:7

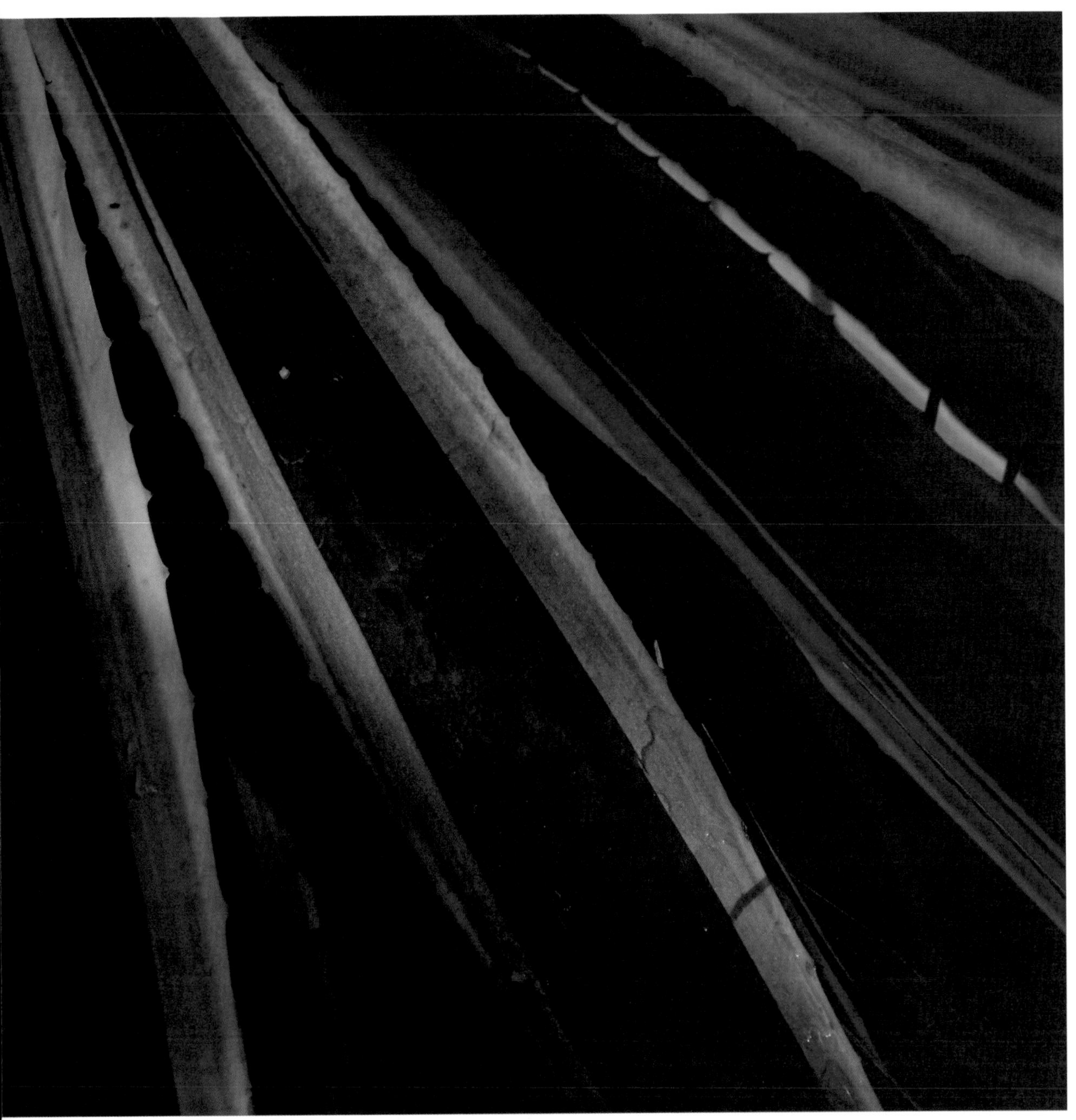

Week Three

DAY TWENTY-ONE

WEEKLY TRUTH

WEEK — THREE

Scripture is God-breathed and true. When we memorize it, we carry His Word with us wherever we go.

For this study, we've been memorizing Psalm 121:1-2. This week, we'll bring the two verses together.

See tips for memorizing Scripture on page 96.

I LIFT MY EYES TOWARD THE MOUNTAINS. WHERE WILL MY HELP COME FROM? MY HELP COMES FROM THE LORD, THE MAKER OF HEAVEN AND EARTH.

PSALM 121:1–2

BENEDICTION

The LORD will protect your coming and going both now and forever.

PSALM 121:8

Tips for Memorizing Scripture

At She Reads Truth, we believe Scripture memorization is an important discipline in your walk with God. Committing God's Truth to memory means He can minister to us—and we can minister to others—through His Word no matter where we are. As you approach the Weekly Truth passage in this book, try these memorization tips to see which techniques work best for you!

STUDY IT

Study the passage in its biblical context, and ask yourself a few questions before you begin to memorize it: What does this passage say? What does it mean? How would I say this in my own words? What does it teach me about God? Understanding what the passage means helps you know why it is important to carry it with you wherever you go.

Break the passage into smaller sections, memorizing a phrase at a time.

PRAY IT

Use the passage you are memorizing as a prompt for prayer.

WRITE IT

Dedicate a notebook to Scripture memorization, and write the passage over and over again.

Diagram the passage after you write it out. Place a square around the verbs, underline the nouns, and circle any adjectives or adverbs. Say the passage aloud several times, emphasizing the verbs as you repeat it. Then do the same thing again with the nouns, then the adjectives and adverbs.

Write out the first letter of each word in the passage somewhere you can reference it throughout the week as you work on your memorization.

Use a whiteboard to write out the passage. Erase a few words at a time as you continue to repeat it aloud. Keep erasing parts of the passage until you have it all committed to memory.

CREATE

If you can, make up a tune for the passage to sing as you go about your day, or try singing it to the tune of a favorite song.

Sketch the passage, visualizing what each phrase would look like in the form of a picture. Or, try using calligraphy or altering the style of your handwriting as you write it out.

Use hand signals or signs to come up with associations for each word or phrase and repeat the movements as you practice.

SAY IT

Repeat the passage out loud to yourself as you are going through the rhythm of your day—getting ready, pouring your coffee, waiting in traffic, or making dinner.

Listen to the passage read aloud to you.

Record a voice memo on your phone and listen to it throughout the day or play it on an audio Bible.

SHARE IT

Memorize the passage with a friend, family member, or mentor. Spontaneously challenge each other to recite the passage, or pick a time to review your passage and practice saying it from memory together.

Send the passage as an encouraging text to a friend, testing yourself as you type to see how much you have memorized so far.

KEEP AT IT!

Set reminders on your phone to prompt you to practice your passage.

Purchase a She Reads Truth Scripture Card Set or keep a stack of note cards with Scripture you are memorizing by your bed. Practice reciting what you've memorized previously before you go to sleep, ending with the passages you are currently learning. If you wake up in the middle of the night, review them again instead of grabbing your phone. Read them out loud before you get out of bed in the morning.

CSB BOOK ABBREVIATIONS

OLD TESTAMENT

GN Genesis
EX Exodus
LV Leviticus
NM Numbers
DT Deuteronomy
JOS Joshua
JDG Judges
RU Ruth
1SM 1 Samuel
2SM 2 Samuel
1KG 1 Kings
2KG 2 Kings
1CH 1 Chronicles
2CH 2 Chronicles
EZR Ezra
NEH Nehemiah
EST Esther
JB Job
PS Psalms
PR Proverbs
EC Ecclesiastes
SG Song of Solomon
IS Isaiah
JR Jeremiah
LM Lamentations
EZK Ezekiel
DN Daniel
HS Hosea
JL Joel
AM Amos
OB Obadiah
JNH Jonah
MC Micah
NAH Nahum
HAB Habakkuk
ZPH Zephaniah
HG Haggai
ZCH Zechariah
MAL Malachi

NEW TESTAMENT

MT Matthew
MK Mark
LK Luke
JN John
AC Acts
RM Romans
1CO 1 Corinthians
2CO 2 Corinthians
GL Galatians
EPH Ephesians
PHP Philippians
COL Colossians
1TH 1 Thessalonians
2TH 2 Thessalonians
1TM 1 Timothy
2TM 2 Timothy
TI Titus
PHM Philemon
HEB Hebrews
JMS James
1PT 1 Peter
2PT 2 Peter
1JN 1 John
2JN 2 John
3JN 3 John
JD Jude
RV Revelation

BIBLIOGRAPHY

Dorsey, David A. *The Roads and Highways of Ancient Israel.* Eugene: Wipf and Stock Publishers, 2018.

MacRae, George W. "Meaning and evolution of the feast of tabernacles." *The Catholic Biblical Quarterly* 22, no. 3. (July 1960): 251–276. Accessed January 26, 2017, with ATLA Religion Database with ATLASerials, EBSCOhost.

Merzger, Bruce M. and Micahel David Coogan. *The Oxford Companion to the Bible.* New York: Oxford University Press, 1993.

Riddle, A. D. "The Passover Pilgrimage from Jericho to Jerusalem," in *Lexham Geographic Commentary on the Gospels*, edited by Barry J. Beitzel and Kristopher A. Lyle. Bellingham: Lexham Press, 2016.

VanderKam, James C. "Covenant and Pentecost." *Calvin Theological Journal* 37, no. 2 (November 2002): 239–254. Accessed January 26, 2017, with ATLA Religion Database with ATLASerials, EBSCOhost.

You just spent 21 days in the Word of God!

MY FAVORITE DAY OF THIS READING PLAN:

HOW DID I FIND DELIGHT IN GOD'S WORD?

ONE THING I LEARNED ABOUT GOD:

WHAT WAS GOD DOING IN MY LIFE DURING THIS STUDY?

WHAT DID I LEARN THAT I WANT TO SHARE WITH SOMEONE ELSE?

A SPECIFIC PASSAGE OR VERSE THAT ENCOURAGED ME:

A SPECIFIC PASSAGE OR VERSE THAT CHALLENGED AND CONVICTED ME: